BASEBALL LEGENDS

Hank Aaron
Grover Cleveland Alexander
Ernie Banks
Johnny Bench
Yogi Berra
Roy Campanella
Roberto Clemente
Ty Cobb
Dizzy Dean
Joe DiMaggio
Bob Feller
Jimmie Foxx
Lou Gehrig
Bob Gibson
Rogers Hornsby
Walter Johnson
Sandy Koufax
Mickey Mantle
Christy Mathewson
Willie Mays
Stan Musial
Satchel Paige
Brooks Robinson
Frank Robinson
Jackie Robinson
Babe Ruth
Duke Snider
Warren Spahn
Willie Stargell
Honus Wagner
Ted Williams
Carl Yastrzemski
Cy Young

CHELSEA HOUSE PUBLISHERS

YOGI BERRA

Marty Appel

Introduction by
Jim Murray

Senior Consultant
Earl Weaver

CHELSEA HOUSE PUBLISHERS
New York • Philadelphia

Published by arrangement with
Chelsea House Publishers.
Newfield Publications is a federally
registered trademark of Newfield
Publications, Inc.

Produced by James Charlton Associates
New York, New York.

Designed by Hudson Studio
Ossining, New York.

Typesetting by LinoGraphics
New York, New York.

Picture research by Carolann Hawkins
Cover illustration by Dan O'Leary

Library of Congress Cataloging-in-Publication Data

Appel, Martin.
    Yogi Berra / Marty Appel ; introduction by Jim Murray ;
  senior consultant, Earl Weaver.
       p.   cm. — (Baseball legends)
    Includes bibliographical references (p.) and index.
    Summary: A biography of one of baseball's greats. Yogi Berra,
  who was player, coach, and manager.
       ISBN 0-7910-1169-0. — ISBN 0-7910-1203-4
    1. Berra, Yogi, 1925–   —Juvenile literature.
    2. Baseball players—United States—Biography—Juvenile
  literature. 3. Baseball—United States—Coaches—Biography—
  Juvenile literature. [1. Berra, Yogi, 1925– . 2. Baseball players.] I.
  Title. II. Series.
  GV865.B4A77 1992   91-16692
  796.357'092B—dc20   CIP
  [B]   AC

CONTENTS

WHAT MAKES A STAR

Jim Murray

No one has ever been able to explain to me the mysterious alchemy that makes one man a .350 hitter and another player, more or less identical in physical makeup, hard put to hit .200. You look at an Al Kaline, who played with the Detroit Tigers from 1953 to 1974. He was pale, stringy, almost poetic-looking. He always seemed to be struggling against a bad case of mononucleosis. But with a bat in his hands, he was King Kong. During his career, he hit 399 home runs, rapped out 3,007 hits, and compiled a .297 batting average.

Form isn't the reason. The first time anybody saw Roberto Clemente step into the batter's box for the Pittsburgh Pirates, the best guess was that Clemente would be back in Double A ball in a week. He had one foot in the bucket and held his bat at an awkward angle—he looked as though he couldn't hit an outside pitch. A lot of other ballplayers may have had a better-looking stance. Yet they never led the National League in hitting in four different years, the way Clemente did.

Not every ballplayer is born with the ability to hit a curveball. Nor is exceptional hand-eye coordination the key to heavy hitting. Big-league locker rooms are filled with players who have all the attributes, save one: discipline. Every baseball man can tell you a story about a pitcher who throws a ball faster than anyone has ever seen but who has no control on or *off* the field.

The Hall of Fame is full of people who transformed themselves into great ballplayers by working at the sport, by studying the game, and making sacrifices. They're overachievers—and winners. If you want to find them, just watch the World Series. Or simply read about New York Yankee great Lou Gehrig; Ted Williams, "the Splendid Splinter" of the Boston Red Sox; or the Dodgers' strikeout king Sandy Koufax.

A pitcher *should* be able to win a lot of ballgames with a 98-miles-per-hour fastball. But what about the pitcher who wins 20 games a year with a fastball so slow that you can catch it with your teeth? Bob Feller of the Cleveland Indians got into the Hall of Fame with a blazing fastball that glowed in the dark. National League star Grover Cleveland Alexander got there with a pitch that took considerably longer to reach the plate; but when it did arrive, the pitch was exactly where Alexander wanted it to be—and the last place the batter expected it to be.

There are probably more players with exceptional ability who didn't make it to the major leagues than there are who did. A number of great hitters, bored with fielding practice, had to be dropped from their team because their home-run production didn't make up for their lapses in the field. And then there are players like Brooks Robinson of the Baltimore Orioles, who made himself into a human vacuum cleaner at third base because he knew that working hard to become an expert fielder would win him a job in the big leagues.

A star is not something that flashes through the sky. That's a comet. Or a meteor. A star is something you can steer ships by. It stays in place and gives off a steady glow; it is fixed, permanent. A star works at being a star.

And that's how you tell a star in baseball. He shows up night after night and takes pride in how brightly he shines. He's Willie Mays running so hard his hat keeps falling off; Ty Cobb sliding to stretch a single into a double; Lou Gehrig, after being fooled in his first two at-bats, belting the next pitch off the light tower because he's taken the time to study the pitcher. Stars never take themselves for granted. That's why they're stars.

1

A SECOND CHANCE

The 1951 season marked Yogi Berra's fifth year as the New York Yankees' catcher. It was a position that did not come naturally to him. But Berra had worked so hard at making himself into a good catcher that this season he seemed likely to win the American League's Most Valuable Player Award.

On the afternoon of September 28, however, Berra had other things on his mind. The Yankees were playing a doubleheader at home against the Boston Red Sox. If Berra and his teammates could take both games, they would win their third pennant in a row.

Allie Reynolds was on the mound for New York in the first game. He had already won 16 games that year. One of the victories he had posted just a few weeks earlier was a no-hitter. And now Reynolds was working on hurling another no-hitter. Only Johnny Vander Meer of the

Berra muffs a pop fly that would have been the last out in Allie Reynolds's no-hitter. "The wind was blowing the ball away from him," Reynolds said. "I hoped to make a grab for it. I was afraid I spiked Yogi on the hand when I jumped over him."

9

Cincinnati Reds had ever pitched two no-hitters in a single season.

Reynolds took the mound for the 9th inning as nearly 40,000 fans cheered him on. He was only three outs away from making baseball history.

Reynolds had been helped all afternoon by Berra, who had been calling a great game. Yogi had been studying the Red Sox batters all season and knew their strengths and their weaknesses. He also knew his own weaknesses behind the plate and had improved tremendously as a catcher.

"Yogi was not a real good catcher the first few years," Reynolds remembered. "He never called the game the way I wanted."

But by this sunny September afternoon, Berra had learned how to call them just right.

The first batter in the 9th inning was pinch-hitter Charlie Maxwell. Reynolds got him out on a grounder. Then Reynolds got too careful with Dom DiMaggio, the brother of Yankees great Joe DiMaggio, and walked him. Johnny Pesky, the fifth-leading hitter in the league, was up next. Reynolds regained his concentration and sent Pesky down on strikes.

The Yankees ace now needed only one more out for a no-hitter. But the next batter was Ted Williams, the American League's toughest hitter. The Sox slugger was batting .320 for the season with 30 home runs. Getting him for the final out was not going to be easy.

As Williams stepped into the batter's box and Reynolds looked at Berra for the sign, the fans rose to their feet, rooting for a no-hitter. Williams swung at the first pitch and popped it up behind home plate.

Berra circled under the ball, ready to make the final putout. Reynolds could see, however, that Berra was having trouble with the wind. Yogi lunged for the ball, which plopped briefly into his mitt and then dropped out, landing on the ground as Yogi fell flat on his face.

Berra later recalled his embarrassment over that awful moment. "I wished I could have crawled into a hole," he admitted.

But the game was not over. Reynolds helped Berra to his feet, then patted him on the rear as a show of support. Allie knew he needed Yogi's help in stopping Williams from breaking up the no-hitter.

Williams swung at the very next pitch, a fastball. Amazingly, he popped up this one foul, too, near the Yankees dugout. Yogi could not believe he had a second chance. Racing over, he settled under the ball, reached out, and made the catch to give Reynolds his second no-hitter.

After the game, more sportswriters wanted to talk to Yogi than to Reynolds. As the catcher sat by his locker, munching on a candy bar and preparing for the second game, which would give the Yankees their third pennant in a row, he was able to laugh about his good luck.

But Yogi Berra knew it had taken more than luck to become one of the top players in the game. He was not blessed with great physical skills. At bat and behind the plate, he did not look very much like a major league baseball player. But Berra had been raised by parents who believed that hard work brought success. And Berra had proved them right. Once he put his mind to playing baseball, he could not be stopped. To the Yankees' good fortune, Yogi Berra made himself into one of the best catchers in the history of the game.

2

THE HILL

Lawrence Peter ("Yogi") Berra was born on May 12, 1925, in St. Louis, Missouri. Both of his parents, Pietro and Paulina Berra, had been born and raised in Malvaglio, a town in northern Italy. Hearing that America was a land of opportunity, they had arrived in the United States in the early 20th century to seek their fortune. They settled in St. Louis.

Larry was Pietro and Paulina's fourth son, after Michael, Johnny, and Tony. A daughter, Josie, was born after Larry. He was called Lawdie by his mom, who spoke only Italian and could not pronounce Larry.

Pietro Berra did not find his fortune in the United States. He had to work hard as a laborer to support his growing family. As soon as Larry was old enough, the youngster began working part-time to help out. For a while, he worked at a coal yard. Then he began to sell newspapers— the *St. Louis Post-Dispatch* and the *Star Times*— for three cents a paper.

Larry ("Yogi") Berra (arrow, center) and teammate Joe Garagiola (arrow, left) as members of the Stags sandlot baseball team.

One of Larry's customers always gave him a nickel for the paper and then told him, "Keep the change." Larry never spoke to the customer except to say, "Thanks," but he knew the man was Joe ("Ducky") Medwick, star outfielder of the St. Louis Cardinals and a future Hall of Famer. Larry had seen Medwick play baseball at Sportsman's Park, the Cardinals' home field, but was too shy to strike up a conversation or ask the star for his autograph.

The largely Italian neighborhood in which Larry lived was known as "the Hill." The Berras lived at 5447 Elizabeth Street. Across the street, at 5446, lived Joe Garagiola and his family. Joe was three years younger than Larry, but the two boys had much in common. They both loved sports and became fast friends.

Every day after school, Larry and Joe played either football, soccer, roller hockey, basketball, or baseball, using whatever equipment they could scrape up. Eventually, they banded together with the other neighborhood boys and started their own baseball team, the Stags Athletic Club. Each member paid 10 cents a month to belong to the club. They would also buy candy bars for three cents and resell them for a nickel, then use the money they had raised to buy bats, balls, and catcher's equipment. There was never enough equipment to go around, however, and when they entered the YMCA League to compete against rival clubs, they often had to borrow gloves from the other team.

Joe Garagiola did most of the catching. Larry played second and third and pitched a little. He threw right-handed but batted left-handed. Garagiola was the third-place hitter for the Stags. Yogi batted fourth.

Sportsman's Park, which was also the home of the American League's St. Louis Browns before the team moved to Baltimore and became the Orioles, sponsored a club for youngsters that permitted them to attend Saturday games for free. The Stags never missed this opportunity to see baseball's biggest stars in action. Most of the boys had dreams of playing big-league ball.

Larry, it seems, did much of his dreaming during school hours. He was not very interested in his studies and was not a particularly good student. At the end of the eighth grade, he decided to quit school and get a full-time job.

Larry's decision to quit school was not that unusual for a teenager in the late 1930s. With the United States suffering through a terrible economic depression, youngsters all over the

Major League baseball was played in Sportman's Park from 1902 until 1966, when it was torn down. The ballpark was home to both the N.L. Cardinals and the A.L. Browns, until the latter team moved its franchise to Baltimore in 1954.

country were leaving school to help support their families.

Larry tried all sorts of jobs, including becoming a boxer. He fought nine times for money, winning eight of his fights. After a while, though, he lost interest in boxing.

Around this time, a teammate of Larry's on the Stags, Jack Maguire (who later played two seasons in the major leagues), saw a movie about India that featured a Hindu spiritual leader, known as a yogi. The yogi in the film sat very silently, reminding Jack of the way Larry sat on the bench during ballgames. Jack nicknamed his friend "Yogi," and the name stuck. From that day on, Larry was called Yogi by his friends in the neighborhood.

Playing sandlot ball in a city with two major league teams had its advantages. Big-league coaches and scouts would often take in a sandlot game to check out the local talent. Sometimes, the sandlot players were even permitted to work out at Sportsman's Park.

Among the Cardinal scouts who watched the games was Jack Maguire's father. He encouraged Yogi, Joe, and his own son to dream about playing in the big leagues. The boys were thrilled to know that someone thought of them as major-league prospects.

Garagiola particularly impressed another Cardinal scout, Dee Walsh. Branch Rickey, who ran the Cardinals, took Walsh's advice and offered Garagiola a contract with the St. Louis organization. Yogi was given a contract, too, but he was not offered a $500 bonus like Garagiola was. This upset Yogi, who was three years older than Joe and thought he was further along as a player.

Maguire told Rickey that it would be hard for Yogi to convince his parents to let him play professional baseball. The very least Rickey could do was give Yogi a signing bonus to soften the news. Rickey responded with an offer of $250.

Under normal circumstances, this might have been enough. In the early 1940s, a lot of players signed without receiving a bonus. But Yogi had his pride.

"No way," he said to Mr. Maguire. "If Joey can get $500, I'm worth $500 too."

Rickey did not agree. So as Joey packed up his baseball gear and headed for Springfield, Missouri, to begin the 1942 season in the minor leagues, Yogi remained in St. Louis to work at a shoe factory. Yogi worked long days at the factory. At night, he played ball, all the while thinking about his missed opportunity and about

Joe Garagiola was a 20-year-old catcher when he started for the Cardinals in the 1946 World Series. In game 4, he tied a rookie record by collecting four hits against the Red Sox.

In this play during a 1942 American Legion game in Nebraska, Berra (left) is tagged out by Los Angeles catcher Gene Mauch. The batter is Ray Steger (center). Mauch eventually played infield in the major leagues and then managed in more games and for more years (26) than anyone in history, except Connie Mack, John McGraw, and Bucky Harris.

his friend Joey, who was playing in the minors.

That fall, the World Series was held in St. Louis for the first time in eight years, pitting the Cardinals against the Yankees. After the Cardinals won the series, Yankees general manager George Weiss sent coach Johnny Schulte, who lived in St. Louis, to check on Berra. Weiss had gotten some good reports on the teenager.

Schulte watched Yogi play. Then he visited the Berra home on Elizabeth Street, making some polite small talk before announcing that the Yankees would pay Larry $90 a month to play for Norfolk in the Class B Piedmont League.

There was a moment of silence in the room.

"And," said Schulte, "we will also give you a $500 bonus for signing with us."

Those words were just what Yogi had been waiting to hear. He accepted the offer. Then he spent the winter working at the shoe factory, eagerly awaiting the day he would report to spring training.

Before Yogi left St. Louis, Branch Rickey, who was now running the Brooklyn Dodgers, sent a telegram to the Berra home. He was willing to offer Yogi "a bonus contract" to sign with the Dodgers. Rickey never said how much of a bonus, and Yogi never asked. He had signed a contract and now belonged to the New York Yankees.

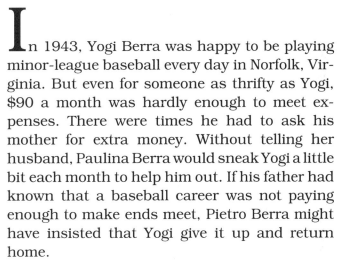

3

A GOOD SPORT

In 1943, Yogi Berra was happy to be playing minor-league baseball every day in Norfolk, Virginia. But even for someone as thrifty as Yogi, $90 a month was hardly enough to meet expenses. There were times he had to ask his mother for extra money. Without telling her husband, Paulina Berra would sneak Yogi a little bit each month to help him out. If his father had known that a baseball career was not paying enough to make ends meet, Pietro Berra might have insisted that Yogi give it up and return home.

One day, discouraged by his low pay, Yogi staged a hunger strike before a ballgame. He told his manager, Shaky Kain, that he could not afford to eat on what he was making. Shaky took pity on his rookie and gave him $2. Yogi quickly filled up on burgers and soda, then went out to play the game.

In game 3 of the 1949 World Series, Berra catches a pop foul hit by Brooklyn's Eddie Miksis. Casey Stengel shouted out instructions to Berra to throw to second to catch Pee Wee Reese trying to advance from first base.

Berra (right) and Bobby Brown (left) congratulate pitcher Tommy Byrne after he pitched a two-hitter against the second-place Tigers in 1949. Brown retired from baseball in 1954 to practice medicine, then returned to the sport 30 years later as the president of the American League.

The $500 bonus would have helped get him through the season, but the money was nowhere to be seen. When Yogi asked about it, he was told, "Oh, that bonus gets paid *after* the season — if you make it through the season."

Yogi never forgot that lesson. He felt misled, and the experience hardened his will. Berra never had much of a formal education, but from that time on he was always smart when it came to negotiating a baseball contract.

As it turned out, Yogi had no trouble making it through the 1943 season. He played in 111 games, hitting 7 home runs and batting .253. Once, Yogi played in two games against Roanoke, Virginia, and got 6 hits in each game, with 13 RBIs in the first game and 10 in the second.

Berra eventually became the Norfolk team's regular catcher that season. He had played the position in St. Louis when Garagiola was not around, and Kain thought that Yogi simply "looked liked a catcher." It was not quite that easy, though. Berra led the league in putouts, but he also led in errors. He was clearly a raw rookie with lots to learn.

But before Yogi could learn any more baseball lessons, he had to serve in the U.S. military. The United States was then fighting in World War II, and most healthy young American men were being drafted into military service. Yogi was no exception. Faced with the prospect of being drafted into the army in 1944, he chose to enlist instead in the navy.

Seaman 2nd Class Lawrence P. Berra was trained to operate machine guns. Then he was shipped off to Europe to fight in the war. There he played a part in one of the war's most important campaigns, the Normandy Invasion. Twice Berra was fired upon, but he was not hit. He later received two medals and several other commendations for his bravery.

In January 1945, Yogi returned to the United States and was assigned to a submarine base in New London, Connecticut. In his spare time, he was able to play ball, both for a navy team and for a local semipro team.

In one exhibition game against the New York Giants, Yogi so impressed Giants manager Mel Ott that his team offered the Yankees $50,000 to purchase the young catcher's contract.

This offer instantly awakened the Yankees' interest in Yogi. If the Giants thought so highly of him, maybe he was a hotter prospect than the Yankees had realized. After all, $50,000 was a lot of money for a 5-foot 8-inch, 195-pound catcher who looked more like a wrestler than a baseball player. Larry MacPhail, part owner of the Yankees, invited Yogi to visit Yankee Stadium.

When Yogi showed up at the Yankee club-house in his navy uniform, Pete Sheehy, the clubhouse manager, asked someone who the stumpy visitor was. When told that Yogi was a player, Sheehy is said to have shaken his head in disbelief before replying, "He doesn't even look like a sailor!"

This would become one of the many stories told about Yogi over the years. Some were true, and many others were invented. Because Yogi did not look like an athlete and had an original way of saying things, he was often teased by sportswriters and players alike. To his credit, he was always a good sport about it. His easygoing nature made him enormously popular with everyone in baseball.

On May 6, 1946, a week before his 21st birthday, Yogi was finally discharged from the navy. He was immediately assigned to the Yankees' top minor-league club, the Newark Bears of the International League, managed by George ("Twinkletoes") Selkirk.

Selkirk already had an exceptional team and did not seem very interested in adding another player to the roster. As a result, Yogi was given a uniform without a number and a cap so small a seam had to be cut open to make it fit on his head.

"Forget this," said Yogi, who was never afraid to speak up. "I'm part of this team. I want a new uniform." And he got it.

Still, Selkirk avoided putting Yogi into the lineup right away. At night Yogi would discuss his lack of playing time and other subjects with his roommate, Bobby Brown. A third baseman, Brown was studying medicine when he was not playing ball. Eventually he became a Yankee infielder as well as a cardiologist. Later in life, he became the president of the American League.

Although Brown was a college man and Berra was an eighth-grade dropout, the two teammates respected each other and became great friends. One night, Yogi is said to have closed the comic book he was reading at the same time Brown closed his medical textbook. Yogi looked over and asked, "How'd *your* book turn out?" It was comments such as this one that endeared

Berra shakes hands with the great Babe Ruth at Sportsman's Park on Babe Ruth Day: June 20, 1948. Ruth, suffering from cancer, died just eight weeks after the tribute.

In a game against the Philadelphia Athletics right after he was brought up to the Yankees in September 1946, Berra tags out Buddy Rosar trying to score.

Berra to Brown and helped create the Yogi legend.

In time, Yogi became the regular Newark catcher. For the season, he knocked out 15 home runs and 59 RBIs in 77 games while batting .314.

When the 1946 International League playoffs ended in September, the Yankees brought up three players—Bobby Brown, pitcher Vic Raschi, and Yogi Berra—for the last few days of the American League season.

Johnny Neun was the Yankee manager when Yogi arrived. In public, he was still called Larry Berra. In fact, for the first five years of his career, he not only signed his autograph Larry Berra but was identified that way by public address announcers and on baseball cards.

In his first major-league start, Berra caught for Spud Chandler, who had been the league's

MVP a few years earlier. Chandler was not at all impressed with Berra as a catcher. The pitcher complained that Yogi's fingers were stubby, and so his signals were hard to see from the mound. Chandler also saw that Berra made it easy for the other team to steal the signs.

Yogi did better at the plate than behind it, hitting a home run in his first game off Philadelphia Athletics pitcher Jesse Flores. Yogi hit another one a few games later. Altogether, he played in seven games and batted .364.

When the Yankees finished a disappointing third that season, it seemed certain that a managerial change would be made during the winter. Yogi hoped that such a change would be to his liking. He had played in only 188 minor league games, interrupted by two years in the navy. His catching was still rough, and no one could remember another batter who swung at so many bad pitches. Yet there was great talent in that ungainly body. It was obvious that Yogi Berra was going to be a very special player.

THE GLORY YEARS

Yogi Berra went home to St. Louis after the 1946 season, just in time to watch his buddy Joe Garagiola star for the Cards in the World Series at Sportsman's Park. Though it was true Yogi would still have to win a job with the Yankees in spring training the next year, Yogi could not help looking ahead to the day when he too would be playing for a world championship.

Yogi soon got his chance. For 1947, the Yankees hired a new manager, Bucky Harris, who had great confidence in Berra. Still, the Yankees knew Yogi needed work as a catcher, so they brought in future Hall of Fame catcher Bill Dickey, who had just retired from the Yankees. Dickey came to spring training to help develop the youngster's skills.

When it came to hitting, Yogi needed no help from anyone. Batting was something that came naturally to him. He had magnificent hand–eye coordination. It was one reason why he became known as such a great "bad-ball hitter." Berra

Three Yankee legends: Yogi Berra (left), Whitey Ford (center), and Mickey Mantle.

had an uncanny ability to make contact on pitches out of the strike zone, fouling them off until he finally got a pitch he could drill. As a result, opponents found the task of pitching to Berra frustrating. He would hit foul ball after foul ball, until they finally had to throw one right over the plate.

By the time spring training was over, Berra was ready for the big time. And the 1947 Yankees were ready for him. They had Joe DiMaggio, the great centerfielder, and shortstop Phil Rizzuto. Among the starting pitchers were Vic Raschi and Allie Reynolds. Joe Page was the team's top reliever. Although the Yankees had not won a pennant since 1943, they were not used to finishing second. The team had won seven pennants and six World Series between 1936 and 1943.

Aaron Robinson did a lot of catching for the Yankees in 1947. He caught 74 games to Berra's 51. But it was obvious to all that Berra belonged in the lineup. Yogi played an additional 24 games in the outfield and wound up batting .280 with 11 home runs. In only 293 times at bat, he knocked in 54 runs.

The Yankees won the pennant easily over the Detroit Tigers, at one point winning 19 straight games to tie the American League record. Then they went on to face the Brooklyn Dodgers for the world championship.

Because both the Yankees and the Dodgers played in New York City, the 1947 World Series created a lot of excitement in New York. Nine million people lived in the city, and for one exciting week it seemed as if every person was a baseball fan.

The Yankees got off to a fast start, winning

the first two games, 5–3 and 10–3. In game 3, which the Dodgers won 9–8, Yogi was asked to pinch-hit against Ralph Branca. He belted the first pinch-hit home run in the 44-year history of the World Series.

The next day, in game 4, Yogi was behind the plate, with Bill Bevens on the mound. Bevens was on the wild side—he walked 10 batters—so not everyone realized that he was on his way to pitching a no-hitter. No one had ever pitched a no-hitter in the World Series. With two outs in the last of the 9th inning, pinch-hitter Cookie Lavagetto belted a double to right that not only ended Bevens's no-hitter but drove in two runs to give the Dodgers a 3-2 victory. Having come within one out of catching a World Series no-hitter, Yogi walked off the field on the losing side.

Casey Stengel (right) talks to Berra, the man he called his "assistant manager." The two had a unique way of describing baseball that often left listeners shaking their heads. Stengel said, "Good pitching will always stop good hitting, and vice-versa," while Yogi observed that "ninety percent of the game is half mental."

Yogi and Carmen Berra at spring training in 1948 just after their honeymoon. When an older fan told Yogi he looked cool in his casual outfit, he replied, "Thank you. You don't look so hot yourself."

Still, the Yankees went on to win the Series, four games to three.

Winning the World Series meant a lot financially to Yogi. Baseball players in the 1940s did not make as much money as they do today. Yogi's rookie salary was $5,000. His winning share for the World Series came to $5,830. In just one week, he more than doubled his earnings.

The next season was not a good one for the Yankees. In 1948, the team fell to third place and Bucky Harris was fired. Yogi, however, continued to improve and became the team's regular catcher. That year, he batted .305 with 98 RBIs and was named to the American League All-Star team.

Harris had been replaced as manager by Casey Stengel, a former outfielder who had managed the Dodgers and the Boston Braves without much success. Stengel was considered by some observers to be a bit too much of a clown for the Yankees. He enjoyed entertaining sports-writers with a kind of doubletalk they called "Stengelese." But he and Berra hit it off from the start. In fact, Berra wound up being the only player to stay with Stengel throughout his 12 years as the Yankees' manager.

As Berra's knowledge of the game and its players grew, Stengel began referring to him as "my assistant manager." It was becoming apparent that Yogi, despite his eighth-grade education, was something of a genius when it came to baseball.

Stengel too, proved to be underrated. While he had never done well as a manager, the truth is he had never before managed a good team. But with the Yankees, Stengel showed he could do the job.

Despite a host of injuries to many key players, the Yankees battled the Red Sox down the wire for the 1949 pennant. On the last day of the season, the two teams were tied. Whichever team won the showdown in Yankee Stadium would be the A.L. champion. The Yankees scored first and held on to beat Boston, 5–3.

Yogi had missed a month of the regular season with a broken finger and played in only 116 games. But he still managed to drive in 91 runs, hit 20 homers, and make the All-Star team. In the World Series, he managed just one hit in 16 at bats. Even so, the Yankees defeated the Dodgers in five games for their twelfth world championship.

A few weeks before spring training began in 1949, Yogi married Carmen Short. His pal Joe

Garagiola served as best man. A few weeks after the 1949 World Series, Yogi returned the favor at Joe's wedding.

Garagiola by this time was developing a reputation as a gifted after-dinner speaker. Much of his material consisted of "Yogi Berra stories," some of which he made up, some of which were true. But they all contributed to establishing Yogi's reputation as a man who unintentionally said funny things. If someone asked Yogi to go to a restaurant for dinner, for example, he might reply, "No one goes there anymore; it's too crowded." Or if someone asked him what time it was, he might respond, "You mean right now?"

As Garagiola's fame grew, more and more people heard his stories. Sometimes Joe would make up long tales that actually had nothing to do with Yogi, but if there was a funny character in the story he would be named Yogi. This practice brought fame to both Joe and Yogi. After Garagiola retired as a player in 1954 and became a sportscaster and later a television show host, the Yogi stories continued. Pretty soon, all America — not only baseball fans—knew of the Yankees catcher.

Yogi was always a great sport. Whenever he was questioned about the funny things he supposedly said, his standard comment was, "I really didn't say everything I said." As usual with Yogi, it made a certain kind of sense.

In 1950, the Yankees were again in a tight pennant race with Boston and Detroit. New York won the A.L. pennant by 1½ games and then beat the Philadelphia Phillies in four straight games to win their third World Series in four years. Yogi had a great year, batting .322 with 28 home runs and driving in 124 runs. He also led the league in putouts and assists. He was clearly the A.L.'s best catcher. His only rival in the majors was Brooklyn's Roy Campanella.

Although Yogi homered in the 1950 World Series against Philadelphia, his lifetime World Series batting average stood at only .140. Eventually, he would become one of the best World Series performers in history, setting records for most Series played (14), most games (75), most times on a winning team (10), most at-bats (259), most hits (71), most singles (49), and a number of fielding records. He would also hit 12 World Series home runs and tie the RBI record with 10 in one World Series, 1956.

In 1951, the Yankees ace Allie Reynolds pitched two no-hitters, but it was Berra who won the Most Valuable Player Award. Six of the top 12 vote-getters for MVP played for the Yanks, but Yogi outpolled them all. He batted .294 with 27

Berra has his arm around pitcher Allie Reynolds (third from right) following Reynolds's second no-hitter in 1951. Nicknamed "Superchief" because he was one-quarter Creek Indian, Reynolds won the Hickock Belt in 1951 as the top professional athlete of the year.

In the early 1950s, the two best catchers in baseball, Yogi Berra of the Yankees and Roy Campanella (right) of the Brooklyn Dodgers, played in the same city. Often World Series rivals, each won three MVP awards between 1951 and 1955.

homers and 88 RBIs — all dropoffs from his previous season—but his work as a catcher was superb, his hitting was timely, and he had the full respect of the sportswriters who voted for the award.

In the 1951 World Series, the Yankees faced the New York Giants, who had won the pennant on Bobby Thomson's dramatic 9th-inning home run against the Dodgers in the N.L. playoffs. The Yankees and the Giants split the first four games, but the Yankees exploded in game 5 to win, 13–1. In the sixth game, the score was 1–1 when Berra began the 6th inning with a single. The hit sparked the team, and before the inning was over the Yankees had a three-run lead. The Giants scored just once more, and the Yankees were the World Champions for the third year in a row.

New York did it again in 1952, edging out the

second-place Cleveland Indians by a single game. Their opponents in the World Series were the crosstown Brooklyn Dodgers, and again the Series was well fought. In the deciding seventh game, the Yankees broke a 2–2 tie in the 6th inning when Mickey Mantle homered. Then relief pitcher Bob Kuzava retired the last eight Brooklyn hitters. The Yankees were World Champions yet again.

Yogi raised his home run output to 30 in the 1952 season, the most ever by a catcher in one season up to that point. Then he clubbed two more in the World Series. Having completed his seventh season, Yogi was by now one of the senior members of the team. He was also a team leader, often batting cleanup and always taking his turn behind the plate, even when he had to play hurt.

Each year from 1950 to 1955 Yogi averaged catching 143 of the 154 regular season games. Reserve catchers Charlie Silvera and Ralph Houk sat in the bullpen day after day, hardly ever getting into a game. What's more, half the catchers on the other American League teams were products of the Yankees' farm system. They had been traded away by the Yankees because Yogi got all of the playing time.

ADDED TRIUMPHS

In 1953, the Yankees again won the pennant. Their opponents in the World Series were the Dodgers, winners of 105 regular-season games. If New York's opponents were familiar, so was the outcome. The Yankees won the first two games, the Dodgers came back to win the third and fourth games, then New York outslugged Brooklyn, 11–7, to win game 5. In game 6, Berra scored the first run on a double and New York took a three-run lead. The Dodgers tied it, 3–3, but the Yankees pushed over a run in the 9th inning to win their record-setting fifth consecutive world championship.

Although the Yankees did not win the pennant in 1954, Yogi won his second Most Valuable Player Award that year. He batted .307 and drove in a career-high 125 runs.

In 1955, the Yankees returned to the top with another pennant and another date with the N.L. champions, the Brooklyn Dodgers. This time, the Dodgers emerged victorious, though it took them seven games to do it. For the first time in history, the world championship went to Brooklyn.

Yogi hit .417 during the Series and won his

The Yankees won the 1953 World Series opener, 9–5, behind the hitting of veterans (left to right) Hank Bauer, Berra, Billy Martin, and Joe Collins. From 1949 through 1953, the Yankees won a record five straight world championships.

third American League MVP Award. He batted .272, belted 27 homers, and drove in 108 runs. Only Jimmie Foxx, Joe DiMaggio, and Stan Musial had ever won three MVP Awards, and no one had won more. Yogi now took his place among the greatest players in baseball history.

Yogi's defense was no longer questioned. Pitchers never shook him off. His finest moment as a catcher was probably in the fifth game of the 1956 World Series, again against the Dodgers. At the time, he was handling Don Larsen, who, like Bill Bevens nine years earlier, was a rather ordinary pitcher having a great day. In game 2, Larsen had been so wild that Casey Stengel had taken him out in the 2nd inning after he had given up a hit and four walks. (The Yankees had taken a 6-run lead in the game after Yogi hit a grand slam home run in the 2nd inning, but the Dodgers came back to win, 13–8.)

Larsen and Berra worked brilliantly together in game 5. They mowed down a tough Brooklyn lineup that included Jackie Robinson, Duke Snider, Roy Campanella, and Pee Wee Reese — all future Hall of Famers. Of the first 26 hitters for the Dodgers, none reached first base. Larsen had to retire only one more player for the last out, pinch-hitter Dale Mitchell. With the count one ball and two strikes, Yogi flashed the sign for a fastball. Larsen wasted no time; he threw it right down the middle for a called strike three. Don Larsen had not only tossed the first no-hitter in World Series history, he had thrown a perfect game. Yogi ran to Larsen and jumped into his arms. Larsen joyfully carried his catcher off the field. For the usually reserved Berra, it was a surprising display of excitement that only added to the special moment.

The 1956 series came down to the seventh game, with the Brooklyn ace Don Newcombe pitted against Johnny Kucks of the Yankees. New York wasted no time in pounding the big Dodgers star, who was named both the N.L. MVP and the first Cy Young Award winner for his season's efforts, and coasted home to a 9–0 victory. The Series hero for the Yankees was Yogi Berra, who batted .360, rapped out 3 homers, and drove in 10 runs. He also shone behind the plate.

If there were still any people around who questioned Yogi's defense, they were hard to find after Berra set a record by playing in 148 consecutive games without an error. Between July

Two of Yogi's three children, Tim (left) and Larry, help their dad polish his trophies in 1954. Larry grew up to play minor-league baseball in the Mets organization, whereas Tim played football as a wide receiver for the Giants and Colts.

An exuberant Berra jumps into the arms of Don Larsen following the last out in Larsen's perfect game in the 1956 World Series. "Fastballs, sliders, slow curves," answered Berra when asked what Larsen threw in the historic game.

1957 and May 1959, Yogi handled 950 chances without making a miscue.

By the end of 1960, the Yankees had won 10 pennants under Casey Stengel, and Yogi had been in 11 World Series. Now approaching his mid-thirties, Yogi was beginning to slow down because of the constant crouching behind the plate. Elston Howard was being groomed to become the team's number one catcher so Yogi could rest his legs and play some games in the outfield.

Berra was the Yankees' left fielder when Bill Mazeroski homered over the left-field wall in Pittsburgh's Forbes Field to give the Pirates a stunning 10-9 win over New York in the 9th inning of the final game of the 1960 World Series. After this defeat, the Yankees fired Stengel.

Ralph Houk, once a backup catcher for Yogi, was named the new manager.

The year 1961 turned out to be Berra's last solid season as a player. Batting .271, he collected 61 RBIs and 22 home runs. As a team, the Yankees hit a record 240 homers, led by Roger Maris's all-time mark of 61 and Mickey Mantle's 54, and won yet another A.L. title. Their opponents in the World Series, the Cincinnati Reds, were no match for the Bronx Bombers. New York won the world title in five games.

In 1962, Yogi Berra played in less than 100 games for the first time since his rookie season, and in 1963 he was a part-time player and first-base coach. By then, he had racked up a grand total of 358 home runs, a record-setting 313 of them as a catcher. Especially impressive was his lifetime total of only 415 strikeouts in 17 full seasons. As a catcher and a hitter, Yogi Berra had done it all. But his baseball career was not yet finished.

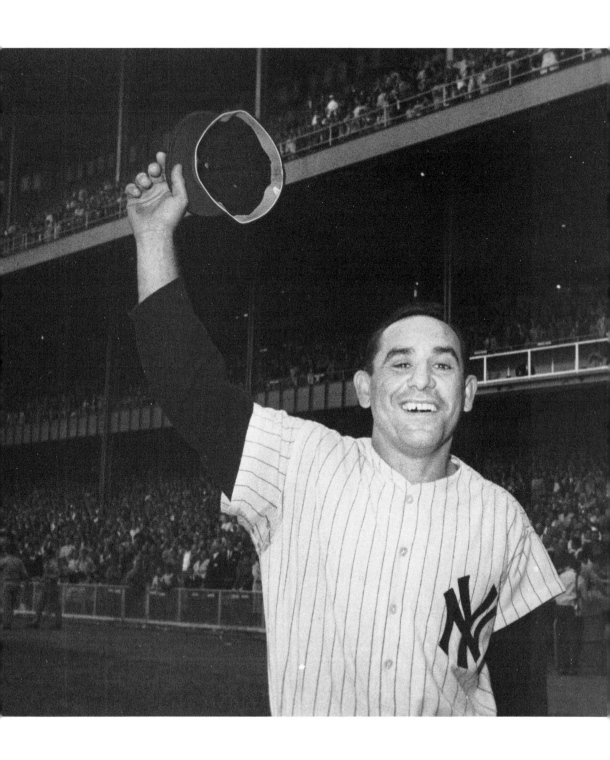

THE MANAGER

Ralph Houk won three pennants in three seasons as Casey Stengel's successor. In 1964, Yankees owners Dan Topping and Del Webb asked Houk to move up to the front office and become the team's general manager. They named Yogi Berra as Houk's replacement.

No one doubted Yogi's knowledge of the game. But most of the experts felt he would have a problem managing the club. He was too nice a guy, some said. Others felt he would have a hard time ordering around players who were his friends and had just been his teammates. Yogi's ability to give the players an occasional pep talk was also questioned. The so-called experts may have had their doubts about the move, but the fans were in favor of it. They loved Yogi. What's more, Casey Stengel was beginning his third season as manager of the New York Mets. The Yankees hoped Berra would help the team draw fans from the Mets.

Berra waves to the fans in Yankee Stadium during the Yogi Berra Day ceremonies before a Red Sox game on September 19, 1959.

The powerful 1961 Yankees featured a record six players who each hit more than 20 home runs. They were (from left to right) Roger Maris (61), Berra (22), Mickey Mantle (54), Elston Howard (21), Bill Skowron (28), and John Blanchard (21). As a team, the 1961 Yankees clubbed 240 home runs, a major-league record.

Yogi took over an aging team that included former teammates Mickey Mantle, Roger Maris, Whitey Ford, Elston Howard, Bobby Richardson, Tony Kubek, and Clete Boyer, as well as young, brash players such as Joe Pepitone, Phil Linz, and Jim Bouton.

The Yankees played poorly for much of the

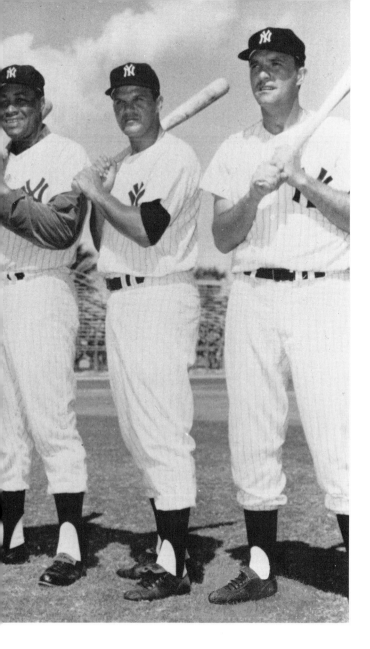

year, but Yogi managed to keep them in contention. One day, the Yankees lost a tough game in Chicago. While riding a bus back to their hotel, Linz took out a harmonica and began to play. Yogi walked to the back of the bus and knocked the harmonica out of Linz's hands. Berra felt that Linz was not taking the loss very hard.

The Yankees were startled by Yogi's rare display of temper, but they respected him for taking the game—and the team—seriously. For the rest of the season, the Yankees played ball the way they were supposed to. Aided by the arrival of rookie pitcher Mel Stottlemyre and veteran reliever Pedro Ramos, they battled the Chicago White Sox and Baltimore Orioles for the 1964 pennant. On October 3, the team finally clinched its fifth-straight pennant.

The World Series brought Yogi to St. Louis to face the Cardinals. Unfortunately, the return home did him little good. The Yankees bowed to St. Louis in a hard-fought seven-game Series.

Within days after the Series ended, Johnny Keane resigned as the Cardinals manager. Yogi Berra was fired. And Keane was hired to replace him.

Yankee fans were outraged by Yogi's firing. After all, he had led his team to the pennant and had come within one game of winning the Series.

As was his way, Yogi did not complain that he had been treated unfairly. It was not his style. He simply returned to his home in New Jersey—where he lived with his wife, Carmen, and three sons, Larry Jr., Tim, and Dale—and waited to see what the future would bring. It turned out to be a short wait.

The New York Mets wasted no time in making Berra an offer he could not refuse: a job on their coaching staff. He would still be wearing number 8 on the back of a New York uniform. Best of all, he would be working with his old friend Casey Stengel.

Stengel did not stick around as manager for long, however. A broken hip forced him to retire in July, and Wes Westrum took over as manager.

This change was fine with Yogi; he liked the former catcher and worked well with Westrum, until he was replaced by Gil Hodges in 1968.

Yogi remained with the team. He was a hard-working coach who tried his best to help the Mets end their run of finishing last or near the bottom every year. After a ninth-place finish in 1968, the Mets stunned the baseball world in 1969 by going all the way to the Series, where they defeated Baltimore in just five games. It was the Mets' first world championship appearance but Yogi's 16th—14 as a player, one as a manager, and now one as a coach. Many theories were offered to explain the team's amazing turn-around. But to old-time New York sports fans, Yogi was clearly the lucky charm.

RETURN TO TRIUMPHS

In January 1972, Yogi Berra was honored with the ultimate award for a baseball player when he was elected to the Baseball Hall of Fame. Later that summer, in ceremonies at Yankee Stadium, the Yankees retired uniform number 8—twice: Once for Bill Dickey, the Hall of Famer who wore the number until he retired in 1947, and again for Yogi, who took Dickey's number when he replaced the catcher.

Less than three months after the Hall of Fame vote, Gil Hodges died of a heart attack. Berra replaced him as manager. The Mets, who had finished fourth in 1970 and 1971, inched their way up to third place under Berra in 1972.

In 1973, the Mets found themselves locked in a tough pennant chase. Although they won only 82 games (they lost 79), which was one game less than their total in 1972, they finished first in their division. Then the Mets triumphed over the mighty Cincinnati Reds to win the N.L. champi-

New York Mets manager Yogi Berra (center) chats with his two top pitchers, Tom Seaver (left) and Jon Matlack (right) before the start of the 1973 N.L. playoffs against the Reds.

In December 1984, a proud
New York Yankees manager
introduced Dale Berra, just
acquired from the Pittsburgh
Pirates. When asked if Dale
had an advantage being the
manager's son, Yogi replied,
"If he hits, he plays. If he
don't hit, he sits."

onship. As a result, Berra was off to the World
Series once again, this time pitted against the
powerful Oakland Athletics, the defending World
Champions.

Berra's team could not hope to match the
power of the Oakland lineup. But the Mets'
strength was their pitchers: Tom Seaver, Jerry
Koosman, Jon Matlack, and Tug McGraw. The
formidable Oakland staff had three 20-game
winners: Ken Holtzman, Jim Hunter, and Vida
Blue. After six games, the series was tied at three
games each. Berra sent Jon Matlack to the
mound for game 7, but Bert Campaneris and
Reggie Jackson each hit two-run homers in the
3rd inning to put the game out of reach. Oakland
won, 5–2, for its second straight World Championship.

The next year, Berra's Mets finished in fifth
place. They started off slightly better in 1975,

but the Mets were not playing well enough to satisfy the team's owners. Berra was fired with two months of the season remaining. For the first time since 1942, he spent August and September at home, out of uniform, out of baseball.

That winter, Berra got a call from Billy Martin, a former teammate and the Yankees' new manager. Martin wanted Yogi to coach the team. Yogi agreed to return. The people who fired him had by now left the Yankees. It was a new era, and the Yankees had a new owner, George Steinbrenner.

The Yankees had not won a pennant since Yogi's dismissal. Some people suggested it was a curse for having fired the beloved Berra. And sure enough, the team won the pennant in 1976—Yogi's first year back—and again in 1977 and 1978. The reasons seemed clear, at least to those who believed in such things.

Over the years, George Steinbrenner changed managers often, but there was always a place for Yogi on the coaching staff. The likable Berra was friendly with whomever managed the team, with the fans, reporters, and all of the stars on the Yankees of the late 1970s and early 1980s. Berra was a contented man. He was coaching the star-ladened Yankees with a good friend as manager of the team. But just when everything seemed in place, the fiery Martin, who had been fired and then rehired twice, was fired yet again by George Steinbrenner.

ONE LAST TIME

W hen Billy Martin was fired for the third time as the Yankees' manager after the 1983 season, the Yankees asked Yogi to run the team.

It had been 20 years since Berra had managed the Yanks. At the age of 58, he led the 1984 Yankees to a third-place finish in the A.L. East with 87 wins. With the addition of pitcher Ed Whitson and base-stealing star Rickey Henderson, Berra was looking forward to a better season in 1985.

Adding to Yogi's enthusiasm for 1985 was the addition of a new infielder the Yankees had acquired in a trade with the Pittsburgh Pirates, Dale Berra. The Berras would be the first father-managing-son pair since Connie Mack and his son Earle worked together for the Philadelphia Athletics more than 70 years earlier.

In the winter of 1984-85, George Steinbrenner announced to the press that "Yogi will be the manager this year, period. A bad start will not

Berra, coach of the Houston Astros, greets then vice-president George Bush in August 1988. In the center is pitcher Nolan Ryan.

affect [his] status either. In the past I have put a lot of pressure on my managers to win at certain times. That will not be the case this spring."

The Yankees got off to a slow start, however, losing 10 of their first 16 games. Concluding that the team was headed for a bad year and completely disregarding his earlier promise, Steinbrenner quickly fired Yogi and brought back Billy Martin as manager.

Berra refused to bad-mouth Steinbrenner in public. But to his friends, he vowed that he would never return to Yankee Stadium as long as Steinbrenner owned the team. Yogi's friends knew he meant it. He did not return for any old-timers' games. In fact, he did not even go back when they dedicated a plaque in his honor at the Stadium in 1988.

After Yogi Berra was fired in 1985, he played a lot of golf and watched baseball on television,

When Berra was fired as the Yankees' manager in 1985, he was replaced by his old friend Billy Martin (right), shown here in 1983. The combative Martin, who died in a car accident in 1989, was no stranger to firings; in addition to being named the Yankees' manager five different times, he managed the Twins, Tigers, and Rangers.

rooting for Dale and cheering for the Yankees. At the age of 60, Berra figured that his baseball career was over. But John McMullen, owner of the Houston Astros and a neighbor of Berra's, offered him a coaching job with the Houston Astros. Yogi accepted the job.

In his first year playing, managing or coaching a team outside New York City, Berra again seemed to be the good luck charm a team needed to win a pennant. In 1986, the Astros finished first in the N.L. West. The team then lost the National League Championship Series in six games to the Mets.

The Astros did not repeat as champions in 1987, but it was a satisfying year for the Berra family. Dale joined the Astros and played in 19 games.

Yogi finally retired from the dugout for good after the 1989 season but still holds a position as Houston's senior baseball advisor.

"It's never over til it's over," Berra was known to say. A player should not give up until the very last out has been made. But for Yogi, the game had finally come to an end.

Even in retirement Yogi Berra remains the favorite of fans everywhere. He is remembered not only for his great playing career but for being one of the game's great characters, a lovable man who had a special way of saying things. He once told the crowd at Yogi Berra Night in St. Louis, "I want to thank all of those who made this night necessary."

As far as his fans are concerned, Yogi Berra is the one who deserves all the thanks.

CHRONOLOGY

May 12, 1925	Born in St. Louis, Missouri
Nov. 11, 1942	Signs with New York Yankees organization
1943	Makes pro debut in Norfolk, Virginia
1944–45	Serves in the Navy during World War II
Sept. 1946	Homers in Major League debut
Oct. 5,1947	Hits the first pinch-hit home run in World Series history
Jan. 26, 1949	Marries Carmen Short in St. Louis
Dec. 8, 1949	First son, Larry Jr., born
Sept. 23, 1951	Second son, Tim, born
Nov. 1951	Wins the A.L. MVP Award
Sept. 1952	Becomes first catcher to hit 30 home runs in a season
Nov. 1954	Wins second MVP award
Nov. 1955	Becomes fourth player ever to win three MVP awards
Sept.5 1956	Ties Gabby Hartnett's all-time home run record for catchers
Oct 8, 1956	Catches Don Larsen's perfect game in World Series
Dec. 13, 1956	Third son, Dale, born
May 10, 1959	Consecutive errorless streak ends at 148 games, a record for catchers
Sept. 19, 1959	Yogi Berra Day at Yankee Stadium
Oct. 1960	Plays in record 11th World Series
1963	Named player-coach for Yankees
Oct. 24, 1963	Named Yankees manager for 1964
Oct. 15, 1964	Yankees lose World Series in seven games
Oct. 16, 1964	Fired as Yankees manager
Nov. 17, 1964	Hired as coach by New York Mets
April 6, 1972	Named manager of Mets
Aug. 7, 1972	Inducted into Baseball Hall of Fame
July 22, 1972	Yankees retire his uniform number, 8
Oct. 21, 1973	Mets lose World Series in seven games
Aug. 6, 1975	Fired as Mets manager
Dec. 5, 1975	Hired as coach by the Yankees
Dec. 16, 1983	Named manager of Yankees
April 28, 1985	Fired by Yankees
1986–1989	Hired as coach by the Houston Astros

LAWRENCE PETER BERRA
"YOGI"
NEW YORK, A. L. 1946-1963
NEW YORK, N. L. 1965

PLAYED ON MORE PENNANT-WINNERS (14) AND
WORLD CHAMPIONS (10) THAN ANY PLAYER IN
HISTORY. HAD 358 HOME RUNS AND LIFETIME
.285 BATTING AVERAGE. SET MANY RECORDS
FOR CATCHERS, INCLUDING 148 CONSECUTIVE
GAMES WITHOUT AN ERROR. VOTED A. L. MOST
VALUABLE PLAYER 1951-54-55. MANAGED
YANKEES TO PENNANT IN 1964.

MAJOR LEAGUE STATISTICS

NEW YORK YANKEES, NEW YORK METS

YEAR	TEAM	G	AB	R	H	2B	3B	HR	RBI	AVG	SB
1946	NY A	7	22	3	8	1	0	2	4	.364	0
1947		83	293	41	82	15	3	11	54	.280	0
1948		125	469	70	143	24	10	14	98	.305	3
1949		116	415	59	115	20	2	20	91	.277	2
1950		151	597	116	192	30	6	28	124	.322	4
1951		141	547	92	161	19	4	27	88	.294	5
1952		142	534	97	146	17	1	30	98	.273	2
1953		137	503	80	149	23	5	27	108	.296	0
1954		151	584	88	179	28	6	22	125	.307	0
1955		147	541	84	147	20	3	27	108	.272	1
1956		140	521	93	155	29	2	30	105	.298	3
1957		134	482	74	121	14	2	24	82	.251	1
1958		122	433	60	115	17	3	22	90	.266	3
1959		131	472	64	134	25	1	19	69	.284	1
1960		120	359	46	99	14	1	15	62	.276	2
1961		119	395	62	107	11	0	22	61	.271	2
1962		86	232	25	52	8	0	10	35	.224	0
1963		64	147	20	43	6	0	8	2	.293	1
1965	NY N	4	9	1	2	0	0	0	0	.222	0
Totals		**2120**	**7555**	**1175**	**2150**	**321**	**49**	**358**	**1430**	**.285**	**30**
World Series (14 years)		75	259	41	71	10	0	12	39	.274	0
All-Star Games (15 years)		15	41	5	8	0	0	1	3	.195	0

FURTHER READING

Berra, Yogi, and Ed Fitzgerald. *Yogi: The Autobiography of a Professional Baseball Player.* New York: Doubleday. 1961.

Berra, Yogi, with Tom Horton. *Yogi: It Ain't Over.* New York: McGraw-Hill. 1989.

Charlton, James. *The Baseball Chronology.* New York: Macmillan, 1991.

Garagiola, Joe. *It's Anybody's Ballgame.* Chicago: Contemporary. 1988.

Okrent, Daniel, and Harris Lewine, eds. *The Ultimate Baseball Book.* Boston: Houghton Mifflin, 1979.

Pepe, Phil. *The Wit and Wisdom of Yogi Berra.* New York: St. Martin's. 1990.

Schoor, Gene. *The Story of Yogi Berra.* New York: Doubleday. 1976.

Trimble, Joe. *Yogi Berra.* New York: A.S. Barnes. 1952.

INDEX

CTURE CREDIT
ational Baseball Library, Cooperstown, NY: pp. 12, 15, 18, 31, 35, 47, 60; UPI/Bettmann: pp. 2, 8, 17, 20, 22, 25, 26, 28, 32,
, 38, 41, 42, 50, 52, 54, 56, 58

MARTY APPEL is the author of 10 books on baseball, including collaborations with Tom Seaver, the late Yankee captain Thurman Munson, and former Baseball Commissioner Bowie Kuhn. His "First Book of Baseball" is one of the top-selling introductory reading books on the sport and a nominee for a Washington Irving Book Award. He is the Emmy Award-winning producer of New York Yankee baseball on WPIX television in New York, and a former Yankee public relations director.

JIM MURRAY, veteran sports columnist of the *Los Angeles Times*, is one of America's most acclaimed writers. He has been named "America's Best Sportswriter" by the National Association of Sportscasters and Sportswriters 14 times, was awarded the Red Smith Award, and was twice winner of the National Headliner Award. In addition, he was awarded the J. G. Taylor Spink Award in 1987 for "meritorious contributions to baseball writing." With this award came his 1988 induction into the National Baseball Hall of Fame in Cooperstown, New York. In 1990, Jim Murray was awarded the Pulitzer Prize for Commentary.

EARL WEAVER is the winningest manager in Baltimore Orioles history by a wide margin. He compiled 1,480 victories in his 17 years at the helm. After managing eight different minor league teams, he was given the chance to lead the Orioles in 1968. Under his leadership the Orioles finished lower than second place in the American League East only four times in 17 years. One of only 12 managers in big league history to have managed in four or more World Series, Earl was named Manager of the Year in 1979. The popular Weaver had his number 4 retired in 1982, joining Brooks Robinson, Frank Robinson, and Jim Palmer, whose numbers were retired previously. Earl Weaver continues his association with the professional baseball scene by writing, broadcasting, and coaching.